BODMIN AND WENFORD RAILWAY

Don Bishop

HALSGROVE

First published in Great Britain in 2011

Copyright © Don Bishop 2011

British Library Cataloguing-in-Publication Data
A CIP record for this title is available from the British Library

ISBN 978 1 84114 921 9

HALSGROVE
Halsgrove House,
Ryelands Business Park,
Bagley Road, Wellington, Somerset TA21 9PZ
Tel: 01823 653777   Fax: 01823 216796
email: sales@halsgrove.com

Part of the Halsgrove group of companies.
Information on all Halsgrove titles is available at: www.halsgrove.com

Printed in Italy by Grafiche Flaminia

CONTENTS

MAP OF THE RAILWAYS AROUND BODMIN

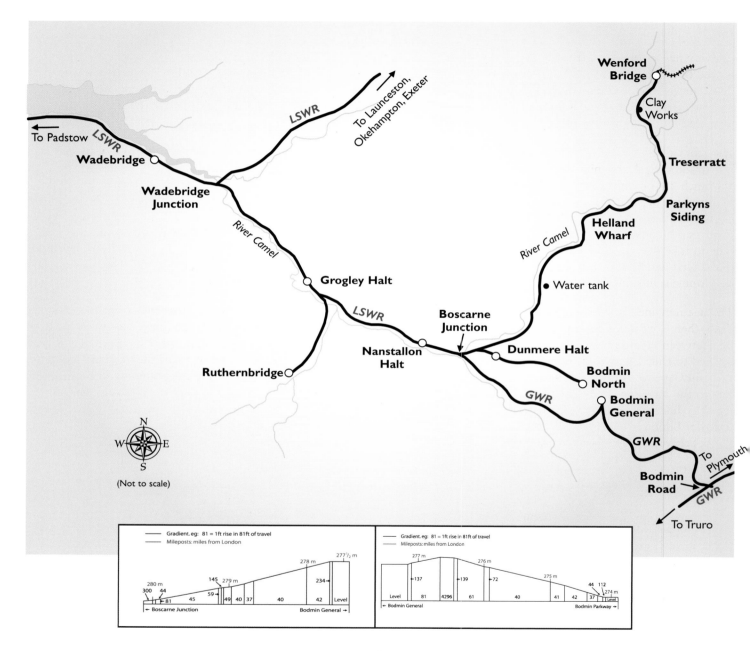

INTRODUCTION AND HISTORY

Most of our heritage railways today try to recreate the past in the local area to some degree. It is possibly easier for some more than others, depending on what is left of the past in that particular area. But the Bodmin and Wenford Railway has managed to recreate the railway history of its local area to a much greater extent than most others and has indeed been labelled as the "National Railway Museum of Cornwall". The line has a superb collection of locomotives that once worked in the county, including one of the famous Beattie Well tanks, a T9 and a 55xx Prairie tank from the steam era and Class 37 and 50 diesels from more recent times. In this book I have set out to show how the steam era has been recreated by the unstinting efforts of the volunteers and staff at Bodmin over the past twenty or so years.

The story of the railways around Bodmin is a very interesting one. Indeed the area was at the forefront of the railway revolution with the opening of the Bodmin and Wadebridge Railway in 1834, between Wadebridge and Wenfordbridge, with a branch to Bodmin (later to become Bodmin North). The line was the brainchild of local landowner Sir William Molesworth of Pencarrow, who had commissioned a study in 1831 to build a railway from Wadebridge to transport sand for use as an agricultural fertilizer. There were very few railways in existence at this time, and none in London, and it was perhaps a big gamble in such an isolated part of the country. The financial pressures soon started to show, and there were bids to take over the line by the broad gauge Cornwall Railway and the Cornwall and Devon Central Railway, but both bids failed and it was not until 1846 that the London and South Western Railway took over the line. This was an odd development in some ways as the LSWR's nearest line was some 200 miles away at this time.

The line remained isolated until 1887 when the LSWR's big rival the Great Western Railway constructed a line into Bodmin itself, then Cornwall's county town, from its Bodmin Road Station at Glynn Bridge on the broad gauge Cornwall Railway line between Plymouth and Falmouth, which had opened in 1859. The line was built to the narrower "standard gauge" and opened to traffic between Bodmin Road and Bodmin General on 27 May 1887. A second line was then constructed from Bodmin General to Boscarne Junction and was opened in September 1888, finally connecting the Bodmin and Wadebridge line to the outside world, albeit via the line's owner's (the LSWR) rival's route! However until the GWR's main Cornwall Railway line was converted from broad to standard gauge in 1892 passengers and goods had to be transferred between trains at Bodmin Road. This physical "separation" also meant the line was worked by dedicated locomotives in those early years, believed to have been two 0-6-0 saddle tanks numbered 1222 and 1224.

The LSWR itself did not complete its link until June 1895, via the new North Cornwall Railway which had been constructed from Okehampton via Launceston to Wadebridge and later extended to Padstow in March 1899.

Traffic settled into a long term pattern, except for a short break between 1886 and 1895 whilst alterations were carried out on the Wadebridge line. The GWR operated its trains between Bodmin Road and Bodmin General and then over the connection down to the LSWR's line at Boscarne Junction, where they had running powers to continue to Wadebridge, but not to call at the intermediate stations that the LSWR had built in 1906. The LSWR operated its services between Padstow, Wadebridge and Bodmin North and out of the area via its North Cornwall line to Launceston, Okehampton and Exeter. Mineral traffic continued on the line between Boscarne Junction and Wenfordbridge. There had also been a short branch to Ruthern Bridge (west of Bodmin), which left the Wadebridge line near Grogley Halt, but this closed in 1933. There was great rivalry between the LSWR and GWR, in particular for through traffic to London and the rest of the country. The LSWR's Bodmin North Station was closer to the town centre than the GWR's "General" Station, and this appeared to work in their favour.

Another development was that the clay companies realised that using the south Cornwall coast port of Fowey, for shipment of their products from the dries at Wenfordbridge, was much better than the smaller and shallower facilities at Wadebridge. Although this would involve trains reversing at Boscarne Junction, Bodmin General and Bodmin Road (!) the benefit of being able to use larger vessels, and thus send to more destinations, was attractive – and to the benefit of the GWR line.

The GWR line was busy in the early 1900s with passengers, general goods, minerals and livestock all being handled, but by the 1930s the figures had halved as the recession bit and the number of omnibuses and lorries increased. Typically there were about 10 trains in each direction through the day, with most but not all, working through to and from Wadebridge. Motive power for many decades was provided by the classic GWR small 45xx and 55xx Prairie tanks. Occasional appearances by Southern 02 class 0-4-4Ts and N class 2-6-0s also occurred.

At Bodmin General, today's preserved station, the GWR provided a goods shed, signal box and engine shed and associated facilities. Most of these were swept away in the name of progress by BR in the 1970s when the line was in use for clay traffic only. However today's Bodmin and Wenford Railway has built a new engine shed, on the site of the original, and built a replica signal box along with the essential workshop facilities required to run a heritage line.

During the war years the line between Bodmin and Wadebridge, and then the North Cornwall line, was used as a diversionary route for trains to avoid Plymouth, and some larger loco types were permitted on the line for this reason.

The LSWR had become part of the larger Southern Railway network at the railway grouping in 1923, the GWR continuing through this period of history as was. In 1948 the railways were nationalised, being in a poor state after the Second World War, and the new British Railways was created.

The old rivalries continued, but changes caused some blurring of control in 1950 when the regional boundaries were changed and the Western Region took over the former Southern Railway lines west of Exeter, only to be transferred back again in 1958 and then finally to the Western again in 1963.

Diesel locomotives, in the form of class 22 diesel hydraulics, and Diesel Multiple Units were tried on the branch and soon replaced steam, the loco shed at Bodmin General closing in April 1962. The DMUs took over all passenger services and the diesel locos only worked goods and clay trains. Changes took place in 1964 that saw a four-wheeled railbus introduced between Boscarne Junction and Bodmin North that connected with the through Wadebridge – Bodmin General – Bodmin Road services at new exchange platforms situated in the "v" between the diverging lines.

With the infamous "Beeching Report" of 1963 came doom and gloom for many branch lines with the increasingly car-owning public shunning such services. In October 1966 the North Cornwall line was closed and on 30 January 1967 services ceased between Bodmin Road, Bodmin General, Wadebridge and Padstow, together with the Bodmin North experiment. The last train was worked by class 22 diesel hydraulic No. D6309. After 133 years Bodmin and Wadebridge were without passenger train services, the GWR branch having lasted just 80 years. Replacement bus services were introduced between Bodmin, Wadebridge and Padstow.

Clay traffic continued to Wenford Bridge, with firstly class 22 diesel hydraulics and then class 25 diesel electrics, then later again class 37s, working the heavier trains up from Boscarne Junction whilst an 08 shunter worked the Boscarne to Wenford section with its tight clearances and curves. The shunter was restricted to eight wagons when it worked trains up the steep 1 in 37 climb from Boscarne Junction to Bodmin General and occasionally onto Bodmin Road. Goods traffic to and from Wadebridge also continued until 2 September 1978, with dust from Delabole Quarry being one of the last traffics carried. The line west of Boscarne Junction was then completely closed and track soon lifted, leaving Boscarne as a reversal point only for the Wenford clay traffic. The clay trains started to run less frequently and in September 1983 these too ceased, resulting in the final closure of the Bodmin line. The signal box at Bodmin Road was subsequently closed, but today survives as the station café. The track was lifted between Boscarne Junction and Wenford Bridge allowing the North Cornwall District Council to convert the whole line between Padstow, Wadebridge and Wenford into the Camel Trail cycle path.

Preservation first arrived in Bodmin in the form of the South West Group of the Great Western Society. When passenger services ceased to Bodmin General the group leased the disused engine shed and based its GWR 0-6-0ST No. 1363 (now at Didcot Railway Centre) and Hawksworth coach No. 7372 at the site and held open days using the adjacent BR sidings. The station building survived as a furniture store and so was reprieved from demolition, but the engine shed and goods shed were subsequently demolished when the GWS left the site and concentrated all efforts on its headquarters at Didcot. The original water tower went with them.

In 1984 the new Bodmin Railway Preservation Society was formed to try and reopen the lines between Bodmin Road, by now renamed "Parkway", and Boscarne where track was still in place. The new Bodmin and Wenford Railway Plc was incorporated in 1985 and a share issue launched to fund the purchase of the line and Bodmin General Station. This was successful and the site at General was developed for the start of passenger services between General and Parkway on 17 June 1990. Passengers could again change trains at Bodmin Road (Parkway) for Bodmin General, although car-borne passengers were discouraged from starting their journeys at that end of the line. Much track work was required between General and Boscarne Junction before trains could be restarted, but this was achieved from 14 August 1996.

Goods traffic also returned to the line when local company Fitzgerald Lighting, on the Walker Lines industrial estate in Bodmin, decided to use rail to ship its products out using an old siding that remained, adjacent to the industrial estate. The trains commenced running in December 1989 with trains of three or four wagons being tripped from this siding down to a transfer siding adjacent to the mainline at Bodmin Parkway by the Bodmin Railway's class 08 or 20 locos, and then taken forward by a BR diesel. Sadly the traffic ceased in July 1991 when BR decided to withdraw its "Wagonload" services, but restarted after rail privatisation with EWS (English Welsh & Scottish Railway Co.) only to cease again July 2001 after a significant rise in charges and the traffic switched over to road haulage.

China clay traffic from Wenford could also have restarted but for the antics of a small but vocal group, calling themselves the Camel Trail Preservation Group. In 1994 it was realised that in excess of 8300 lorry journeys annually could be removed from Cornwall's narrow roads by putting the clay traffic from Wenford back onto the railway. A public enquiry in Bodmin in February 1996 ruled against the railway, however the then Secretary of State overturned the decision in November 1996 and granted the required Light Railway Order. Despite the trackbed not being an official public right of way the vocal opponents forced a judicial review and the LRO was again overturned. At this point the North Cornwall District Council, who had previously been in support of the scheme changed its mind and turned against the rail reinstatement. Subsequently

English China Clays decided to abandon the Wenford site and so the need for the railway disappeared – might it not have done so if the path to reopening had been easier?

Today the line still runs from the original branch platform at Bodmin Road (Parkway); although the platform buildings and canopy have long since been replaced the covered GWR footbridge does survive. The railway company has built an impressive stock storage shed on the sidings to the west of the branch junction adjacent to the connection with the Network Rail mainline. The branch then climbs steeply around a sharp curve over a viaduct and heads up the valley towards Bodmin itself, passing the delightful halt at Colesloggett before continuing at a ruling gradient of 1 in 37 under the A30 dual carriageway to the summit just before the Walker Lines industrial estate and sidings. It then descends slightly into Bodmin General Station. The other leg of the current line bears away behind arriving trains to the left and descends to Boscarne Junction again on a steep gradient of 1 in 40 passing the residential areas of Bodmin and then crosses the River Camel on its final approach to Boscarne where a new station has been constructed. The route onwards towards Wadebridge can be clearly seen beyond the buffer stops at Boscarne and at the other end of the site the Camel Trial footpath/cycle way clearly marks the routes towards Bodmin North and Wenford.

So today's Bodmin and Wenford Railway continues a long and fascinating history of steam worked railways in mid Cornwall and has developed facilities over the past twenty years to maintain and overhaul its fleet of steam and diesel locomotives and rolling stock. Developments continue with the commissioning of the new signalling at Bodmin General due to occur early in the 2011 season allowing two train operation for the first time. Growing passenger numbers mean that the railway's facilities need to be constantly improved and this is being achieved by the loyal staff and volunteers of this friendly little heritage line. Special events are regularly held to demonstrate different themes of Cornwall's railway history. There are still desires to one day extend the line back to Wadebridge, but this would require a completely new station and site at that end of any new line, which would prove costly, as the original one has been redeveloped. But who knows – perhaps one day the funds will be forthcoming and we will once again see a Beattie Well tank, T9 and Prairie tank at work side by side in Wadebridge.

Whilst the majority of the images in this book are my own work I am very grateful to fellow linesiders Bernard Mills and Steve Andrews (Classic Traction) for allowing the use of a small number of their images to tell more of the story of the Bodmin line in preservation. These images have been credited as appropriate in the book. Thanks Guys.

Don Bishop
West Huntspill
February 2011

1. BR STEAM DAYS

Although most of our heritage lines have done an excellent job at recreating the feel of the past steam scene, the Bodmin Railway among them, there are inevitable changes that have occurred since the final days of BR steam. Bodmin Road Station, now Parkway, is a classic case in point with many of the platform structures now demolished in the name of "progress". In this image we see small Prairie tank No. 4552 standing at the Bodmin branch platform with a train for Bodmin General and Wadebridge in September 1960. Note the platform canopy with the footbridge steps built within. *Colour Rail 322120*

At Bodmin General the scene is a very familiar one to that we can see today from the footbridge at the Beacon Road bridge. However note the goods shed in the right background and the original single road engine shed behind the first carriage in the centre of the picture – demolished by BR and now replaced by the railway's two road facility. Small Prairie No. 4559 sets out from Bodmin General with a two coach "B set" towards Boscarne Junction and Wadebridge. *Colour Rail 322123*

Approaching the Beacon Road bridge from the opposite direction is No. 4569 with a classic two coach "B set" in BR red livery from Wadebridge in September 1958. Another view that looks much the same today. *Colour Rail/Trevor Owen BRW474*

We now arrive at Boscarne Junction in June 1964 and see Ivatt 2-62T No. 41272 with a train for Bodmin North running through the exchange sidings. Note the wagons in the siding on the right having been worked up from Wenford Bridge earlier. *Ivor Hocking/Bernard Mills collection.*

Here we see the long gone LSWR station at Bodmin North with Ivatt 2-6-2T No. 41272 running round its train of Southern Maunsell design stock in June 1964. The station buildings and canopy have received a repaint into Western Region Brown and Cream livery following the regional boundary changes in 1963. The Bodmin Gaol is prominent in the background. *Ivor Hocking/Bernard Mills collection.*

On the Wenford branch is Dunmere crossing over what is now the A389 Wadebridge road; the rails in the road still exist although the rest of the branch has of course been long lifted. Here the now preserved Beattie well tank No. 30587 is seen being hand signalled across the road with a train of clay wagons in 1962. *Ivor Hocking/Bernard Mills collection.*

The Bodmin Railway's preserved Beattie tank No. 30587 is seen in 1962 at Wenford Bridge shunting the day's wagons alongside the clay dries. Enthusiasts who had travelled up the line in an extra brake van by arrangement look on. It was to here that the Bodmin Railway had hoped to reopen but local opposition prevented this happening and the clay dries eventually closed. *Ivor Hocking/Bernard Mills collection.*

2. BR DIESEL DAYS

As the end of steam in the West Country arrived the branch lines that were still open were worked by diesel multiple units or the small German-built Railbuses that BR trialled on some lines, including those in the Bodmin area. Little more than a bus chassis on four rail wheels these units didn't last long in BR service as more branch lines closed. One of these four-wheel Railbuses is seen at Bodmin Road in December 1967. Note the surviving water tank and shoot across the branch tracks to the mainline platform. *Bernard Mills*

A single car Diesel Railcar (quite a step up from the Railbus!) leaves Bodmin General and heads away towards Bodmin Road in January 1967. Note the wagons stabled in the "Barracks siding" that has a liberal coating of rust on the rails. *Bernard Mills*

A fascinating image that shows the short lived exchange platforms at Boscarne Junction. The wooden platform on the right had been constructed alongside the former GWR line from Bodmin General to Boscarne (and Wadebridge), which as the running in board proclaims allows passengers to change for Dunmere and Bodmin North. On alighting passengers proceeded along the short walkway, marked by the three lamps posts, to the level platform alongside the former LSWR line to Bodmin North where they could climb aboard the four-wheel Railbus, seen standing at the platform, by use of the vehicle's steps. Quite why it was justified to construct this facility for passengers to change trains here to go to Bodmin North (Dunmere Halt maybe!) when their train to/from Wadebridge was calling at Bodmin General anyway is mystifying. Note the LSWR lattice post signals, in particular the rare "double sided" one on the right of the picture. December 1966. *Bernard Mills*

A view from the west end of Boscarne Junction sidings in December 1967 as a German-built Railbus runs onto the Bodmin North line from the Wadebridge direction. The exchange platforms referred to in the previous caption are at the far end of the sidings where the signals can just be seen. Today's Boscarne Junction station platform is located approx half way along the sidings on the alignment of the track (third from right) the Railbus is heading onto. Note the white china clay wagons stabled in the sidings probably having been tripped from Wenford Bridge. *Bernard Mills*

A good general view of Boscarne Junction taken from the top of the bracket signal in December 1966 which shows the signal box and railway cottage in the foreground, and the four tracks of which the second from left is the Bodmin North line and the one on the right is the Bodmin General line which join together to become the single line to Wadebridge. The Railbus can just be seen waiting at the exchange platform in the distance as can the Ground Frame at the east end of the yard. *Bernard Mills*

A rather tired-looking Bodmin North Station seen in June 1966 with a Railbus waiting for its next departure to the exchange platform at Boscarne Junction. Note the rusting and truncated sidings in the foreground. *Bernard Mills*

A BR Class 03 diesel shunter, No. D2127, employed on the Wenford goods at Dunmere Crossing in June 1966 waiting for the guard to hand signal across the main Wadebridge road. These diesel shunters only worked the Wenford services for a short time after the end of steam before the larger class 08s took over and tripped wagons back to Boscarne Junction where larger mainline diesels worked them forward.
Bernard Mills

BR ran a final farewell train to the Wadebridge line for enthusiasts on 30 September 1978 behind Class 25 No. 25080. The train is seen here passing the derelict wooden exchange platform at Boscarne Junction complete with a farewell wreath. Note that the tall double-sided lattice post signal has been replaced by a more rudimentary stop and await instructions "signal". *Bernard Mills*

3. EARLY PRESERVATION

The first signs of preservation at Bodmin were when the South West Group of the Great Western Society rented the former engine shed at Bodmin General from BR after passenger services had ceased. They held occasional open days in the sidings at Bodmin General, and on one such occasion GWR 0-6-0ST No. 1363 is seen together with preserved Hawksworth coach No. 7372. *Bernard Mills*

With a rather tongue-in-cheek over the top set of headcode and express lamp code, No. 1363 runs alongside the platform at Bodmin General in May 1971. The engine had been allocated to Plymouth Laira shed in BR days so was a relative local. The Great Western Society later vacated the site and concentrated all its resources on its new headquarters at Didcot, Oxfordshire. The engine shed and goods shed (seen behind No. 1363) were subsequently demolished by BR. *Bernard Mills*

The current Bodmin and Wenford Railway started operations in June 1990 between Bodmin General and Bodmin Parkway. In early days they had to rely on the services of a few small industrial locomotives to haul services, but most of these found hauling the trains rather hard work with the steep gradients. One of the locomotives employed, and still owned by the railway today, was former Plymouth Devonport Dockyard shunter No. 19, seen here working hard up the gradient under the three arch bridge, near the A30 road, with a single coach forming the 14.20 ex Bodmin Parkway on 31 May 1991. *Bernard Mills*

On the warm afternoon of 31 May 1991 No.19 works up grade past Charlies Gate with the 17.00 ex Bodmin Parkway. *Bernard Mills*

Three years later on (31 May 1994) 0-6-0 Austerity saddle tank "Swiftsure" hauls a Bodmin Parkway to Bodmin General service past Charlies Gate. The train now made up of three coaches, all in different liveries!

Another view of "Swiftsure" on the warm afternoon of 31 May 1994 working its way uphill under the three arch bridge with rhododendrons lining the cutting sides.

4. THE BODMIN BRANCH TODAY

Starting at the extreme east end of the branch at Bodmin Parkway, compare this view with that on page 13. Alterations have taken place to the ends of the mainline platform and gone is the water tank and shoot across the branch tracks. Considerable tree growth has also occurred. Prairie No. 5552 runs round its train at Bodmin Parkway on 15 October 2009.

Opposite: Another comparison view, this time with that on the top of page 9 which shows that the station canopy and waiting rooms have disappeared and considerable tree growth has occurred around the area. This view shows home based 55xx Prairie No. 5552 having run round its train and now standing at the branch platform with a train for Bodmin General. There are few places on the national network today where you can step off a mainline high speed train and cross the platform to connect with a steam hauled branch train to the nearby market town.

This view of the recently restored T9 4-4-0 No. 30120 leaving Bodmin Parkway reveals that the covered footbridge at the station survives and that a modern waiting room has been provided on the mainline "up" platform. The former signal box, visible on the down mainline platform is now a café run by the Bodmin Railway. 21 October 2010.

This image compares well with that on page 9 *(bottom)* and shows that the main track layout is still largely as was in BR days but the goods shed in the background has gone and the engine shed has been rebuilt as a two road facility following the demolition of the original by BR. The coach visible on the far left is the camping coach accommodation for volunteers. 1948 BR-built large Prairie No. 4160, from the West Somerset Railway, is seen shunting a fruit van into the sidings from Beacon Road bridge on 1 September 2006.

The "new" shed at
Bodmin General with
T9 No. 30120 and
visiting Beattie well tank
No. 30585 (from
Buckinghamshire
Railway Centre) standing
in residence on the
evening of 21 October
2010.

Birmingham Railway
Museum-based Pannier
No. 7752 stands at Boscarne
Junction with a goods
charter on 3 October 1994.
Note the rationalisation of
the site with only two tracks
remaining and the line to
Wadebridge lifted completely
beyond the buffer stops in
the background.

28

The new platform waiting shelter at Boscarne Junction completed in local stone with nice appropriate Southern Region feel.

The current very smart Carmine and Cream-liveried coaching stock of the Bodmin Railway is seen passing Westheath Road behind Prairies Nos. 5521 and 5552 on the climb from Boscarne to Bodmin General on 18 April 2010.

5. 5552 – THE HOME BASED PRAIRIE

The Bodmin Railway's own small Prairie tank No. 5552 has proved a valuable and popular performer on the line in recent years. The engine formally worked in Cornwall during its "service life" so is right at home on the Bodmin line. Here the engine heads a goods train along the "Quarry straight" on 15 October 2009.

Opposite: A two coach local train formation is taken past Kirland on the climb from Boscarne by No. 5552 on 1 September 2006.

No. 5552 is fitted with a taller safety valve bonnet than many of its preserved class mates, and this is clearly visible in this shot of it near Westheath Road with a goods working on 15 October 2009.

6. AUTOTRAINS

A dark threatening sky overshadows 14xx autotank No. 1450 and its autocoach leaving Boscarne on a photo charter working on 13 May 1997.

Collett 14xx tank No. 1450 heading a single autocoach in BR Red/Cream livery of the early 1950s across the River Camel bridge at Boscarne on 13 May 1997.

Opposite: Auto Pannier No.6435 and the line's newly restored autocoach No.W232 passing Charlies Gate on the morning of 10 May 2011.

7. CHINA CLAY TRAINS

A classic type of train seen over very many years in Cornwall, indeed modern air braked versions are still at work in the Duchy today, is the china clay train. Many clay works and dries provided traffic to the railways of Cornwall with trip freights between local facilities and the ports of Falmouth and Fowey and out of the county to other parts of the UK. In steam and earlier diesel days the trains were formed of four-wheel open wagons which were often white with clay residue. The Bodmin Railway has preserved a short rake of these wagons and they are seen here behind No. 5552 climbing past Charlies Gate recreating a scene once so common in Cornwall in the 1950s/'60s. 18 October 2003.

In another scene at Charlies Gate we see visiting 55xx Prairie No. 5526 from the South Devon Railway heading a mixed goods with four clay wagons at the front. Clay wagons were often tripped between locations around the county as part of mixed goods trains. Note the plain BR Black livery in comparison with the line's own No. 5552 in lined green livery.

The Western didn't have all the clay traffic of course, and the famous Wenford clay dries were one of the main sources of traffic that kept the former LSWR line from Boscarne Junction to Wenford Bridge, and its diminutive Beattie Well tanks in service. Indeed there were hopes to reopen the Wenford line to clay trains in the 1990s, post preservation, but these hopes were dashed by local opposition and the dries at Wenford eventually closed. Here a recreation of a short clay train with Beattie Well tank No. 30587 is seen at Bodmin Parkway on 24 March 2003.

After the Beattie Well tanks had been withdrawn in 1962 there was a short period when former GWR 13xx Dock Pannier tanks were used on the Wenford line before dieselisation. On 6 September 1996 the South Devon Railway's No. 1369 is seen glinting strongly as it climbs the gradient near Colesloggett with a train of clay empties.

Trains of loaded clay wagons from Wenford were often left in the sidings at Boscarne and collected later by a Western Region loco and tripped up to Bodmin General and then onwards to Fowey Docks for shipment. Due to the steep gradients on the Bodmin line, train lengths were limited behind the usual Prairie tank locomotives. Here such a train is recreated with No. 5552 getting away from Boscarne Junction with a clay train on 18 October 2003.

Further up the climb from Boscarne Junction, at Westheath Road, No. 5552 is seen with an alternative formation of five clay wagons with the addition of two box vans and on this occasion a former GWR "Toad" brake van. 15 October 2009.

There is no doubt that today's Bodmin and Wenford Railway is able to recreate many classic scenes of Cornwall's railways from the past. Perhaps none better than capturing the look and feel of the Wenford line itself with the little Beattie 2-4-0 Well tanks. Here No. 30587 takes a short mixed goods, including clay wagons, past Charlies Gate on the glorious spring afternoon of 10 April 2005.

8. PANNIER TANKS

The railway's own 57xx class Pannier No. 4612 works hard past Charlies Gate with an afternoon passenger train from Bodmin Parkway to General on 18 April 2010.

The GWR built a good number of varieties of 0-6-0 Pannier tank. One of the smaller ones was the 13xx dock tanks built for use on the Weymouth Quay tramway. When this work was dieselised in the early 1960s three of the class were transferred to Wadebridge shed to replace the ageing Beattie tanks. One of these No. 1369 survived the cutter's torch and today resides at the South Devon Railway. On 6 September 1996 it is seen leaving Boscarne Junction with a photo charter goods whilst on a visit to the Bodmin line.

Opposite: The GWR also built a number of Panniers for use on autotrains and 3 of the 64xx class have survived into preservation. One of these, No. 6435 has recently been purchased by the Bodmin Railway from the Torbay and Dartmouth Railway and is shown here rounding Quarry curve, piloting Prairie No. 5521, on a Bodmin Parkway to Bodmin General service on 18 April 2010.

In September 1995 it was the turn of 57xx class Pannier No. 7714 from the Severn Valley Railway for the autumn gala weekend. I also hired this engine for a day's photo charter and it is seen here leaving Boscarne with a goods train early on 15 September 1995.

Opposite: A bucolic branch line scene, as a wonderful array of wild spring flowers on the lineside at Westheath Road greets Pannier No.4666, 4612 in disguise as a former local engine, with a goods on 9 May 2011.

9. BODMIN ROAD

The connecting service for Bodmin General waits at the branch platform at Bodmin Parkway (Road) behind No. 5552 on 15 October 2009. Note the railway's impressive advertising hoarding on the left featuring No. 5552 itself.

The graceful lines of the LSWR T9 4-4-0 are shown to good effect as No. 30120 gets away from Bodmin Road (I much prefer that name to Parkway!) with a photo charter on 7 October 2010.

Opposite: The two surviving Beattie Well tanks, Nos. 30585 and 30587, make a fussy start from Bodmin Road with a service to Bodmin General and Boscarne on 27 December 2008.

More in keeping and doing the work for which it was intended in Cornwall, No. 30587 is shunting a goods charter at Bodmin Road on 16 October 2009.

10. PHOTO CHARTERS

Opposite: Early morning lighting glows off the train and surrounding trees as a clay train departs Boscarne Junction for Bodmin General behind No. 5552 on 18 October 2003.

Another early morning at Boscarne produces an autotrain headed by Mike Little's 14xx tank No. 1450 on 18 May 1997.

Recent cutting back at Charlies Gate has enabled an early morning shot to be taken on the east side of the line there as an alternative to taking the charter train down to Boscarne Junction first thing. In this view on 19 April 2010 we see the South Devon Railway-based BR Black Prairie No. 5526 with a mixed goods working including the usual china clay wagons.

Another small Prairie visiting the line was the West Somerset Railway's No. 4561 in September 1996. Some recent cutting back at the time allowed this shot near Colesloggett to be obtained (no longer possible due to re-growth) on 5 September, of the engine heading a two coach Maroon passenger train along the branch.

A vigorous climb of the gradient at Cutmadoc is made by Pannier No. 6435 and its autocoach on 10 May 2011.

Another early morning photo charter shot, this time with the T9 No. 30120 leaving Bodmin Parkway in atmospheric autumn conditions on 7 October 2010.

This time we have been lucky enough to catch some glorious evening light at Westheath Road for another shot of the T9 climbing up from Boscarne with a train formed of two Red/Cream coaches but with vans added to each end of the formation as was often the case in the 1950s. 21 October 2010.

11. PANNIER – 4612

The home based 57xx Pannier No. 4612 is seen passing over a carpet of blue "forget-me-nots" on the track at Westheath Road with a train from Boscarne Junction on 18 April 2010. 4612 was built to a design by GWR Chief Engineer C.B. Collett of 1929 and was outshopped from Swindon Works in 1942. The engine is due to be withdrawn for a full ten-yearly overhaul in 2011.

The hazards of railway photography – a generally bright sunny scene is suddenly dulled as a cloud goes over the sun just the train passes by my camera position! No. 4612 passing Westheath Road with a Boscarne Junction to Bodmin General train on 17 September 2009.

12. PRAIRIE TANKS

The railway's own small 55xx Prairie No. 5552 has been a stalwart of services on the Bodmin line for a good number of years and was also once a Cornwall-based engine in BR days and worked on the branch in its "service life". The engine was built at Swindon in 1928 and was allocated to Newton Abbot from 1937 often working trains on the Kingsbridge branch before transfer to Truro in 1955. She was withdrawn from service in October 1960 and then spent 25 years rusting in Barry scrapyard, South Wales until rescue and was returned to steam in 2003. Here the engine works the railway's then Maroon-liveried passenger set past Charlies Gate on 10 April 2005.

There are two varieties of small Prairie tank, the 45xx type with flat topped side tanks and the 55xx type (although actually numbered from No. 4575 onwards) with slightly larger tanks with sloping top. The flat topped variety is represented here by the West Somerset Railway's No. 4561 climbing the bank at Westheath with a photo charter on 5 September 1996.

Opposite: There are 14 small Prairie tanks preserved, three of the 45xx series and 11 of the 55xx series, all bar one having been rescued from the famous Woodhams scrapyard in Barry, South Wales. The example shown here, No. 5526, is based at the South Devon Railway and is currently in plain BR Black livery. Whilst on a visit to the Bodmin line the engine is seen heading a goods charter through Dreason cutting on 19 April 2010.

Opposite: The GWR also had a large fleet of larger Prairie (the name refers to the wheel arrangement of 2-6-2) tanks, and No. 4160 from the West Somerset Railway represents the type here at Bodmin General on 1 September 2006. This loco was built at Swindon works in 1948 so is actually a BR-built loco to a GWR design. There are ten of the 4100/5100 classes in preservation.

Another view at the popular location near Westheath Road, Bodmin showing No. 5552 climbing the steep gradient with a three-coach train from Boscarne Junction on 27 December 2008. The Mk.2 coach on the rear of the train has since been sold off from the railway which now concentrates on MK.1 vehicles which are more in keeping with the heritage steam image.

The flat top tanks of No. 4561 show up well in this back-lit glint shot of the engine climbing to Bodmin General near Colesloggett on 5 September 1996.

13. BODMIN GENERAL

A good general view of the current layout at Bodmin General on a cold winter's day in January 2010. One of the Beattie tanks can be seen at the platform waiting to depart for Boscarne Junction.

There are few signs in this picture that it is in the preservation era... No. 5552 arrives at Bodmin General past the signal box and some stabled wagons in the sidings on 15 October 2009.

The National Railway Museum's Bodmin-based Beattie tank No. 30587 shunting wagons at Bodmin General on 16 October 2009. Note the signals in the background with white crosses on them to indicate that they are not yet in use – the installation was fully commissioned on 19 April 2011.

A classic former Wadebridge pairing of Beattie tank No. 30585 and T9 No. 30120 at Bodmin General on
2 September 2010.

14. BOSCARNE JUNCTION

Boscarne Junction in preservation with one of its old friends in 13xx Pannier tank No. 1369 which worked the Wadebridge to Wenford Bridge goods trains from 1962, following withdrawal of the Beattie tanks after over 60 years service in Cornwall. No. 1369 is seen working a short goods along the sidings at Boscarne before the new station was built. 6 September 1996.

A short while later No. 1369 is seen making a vigorous departure from Boscarne with its short train of four open wagons and brake van.

Opposite: Taking a step back in time for our next recreation as Beattie Well tank No. 30587 works a short goods away from Boscarne Junction platform on 16 October 2009. For such a remote spot Boscarne Junction really does have a very rich history.

Opposite: Keeping with the Southern Region theme for a moment we witness the wonderfully graceful T9 No. 30120 striding out from Boscarne across the River Camel bridge with a photo charter on 21 October 2010.

A warm autumn day makes the exhaust disappear from the T9 as it gets away from Boscarne on 7 October 2010 with another photo charter.

45xx tank No. 4561 in a scruffy
GWR Green livery crosses the River
Camel bridge amid the trees on
6 September 1996.

15. 1369 – THE WENFORD REPLACEMENT

Built at Swindon in February 1934 these little Pannier tanks with just 3ft 8" driving wheels and short wheelbase were designed for shunting in yards and on dock branches where tight curvature was an issue, including the famous Weymouth Quay branch. Of the six locomotives three were based at Swindon (including 1369) and three at Weymouth, although by 1958 one of the Weymouth engines had been moved to Taunton. No. 1369 was moved to Weymouth in 1960 and remained on quay branch duties until dieselisation arrived at Weymouth in 1962. The three engines were transferred to Wadebridge to replace the Beattie Well tanks and remained in traffic until November 1964. It seems that No. 1369 was the regular Wenford engine being the best of the three, 1368 was often shunting at Wadebridge whereas 1367 appears to have worked very little. Here No. 1369 is seen catching a glint from the setting sun at Quarry curve on a photo charter on 6 September 1996.

Preservation for No. 1369 came about following its participation on a railtour on the Wenford line in 1964. It was privately purchased and transferred to the Great Western Society who then had a base at Totnes Quay. The engine had travelled from Wadebridge to Totnes under its own steam becoming the last engine to steam in Cornwall under BR ownership, it being handed to its new owners on arrival at Totnes. Later the engine was transferred to the Dart Valley Railway Co. and saw limited use on the Ashburton branch in the late '60s before repairs resulted in it being stored. It was to be another 24 years before it returned to steam on what had by then become the South Devon Railway. It was restored initially in BR Black livery and was a popular visitor to several locations around the country, including a return to Cornwall and the Bodmin line in 1996. Here the engine works its goods charter way from Boscarne across the River Camel bridge on 6 September 1996.

Another view of No. 1369 back "home" at Boscarne Junction with its charter goods on 6 September 1996. The engine has since been overhauled and retuned to traffic in GWR Green livery and is currently in service at the SDR.

16. BEATTIE WELL TANKS

The predecessors of the GWR 13xx class tanks on the Wenford Bridge line were, as mentioned earlier in the book, three of the former LSWR Beattie Well tanks. The original class of 85 engines were built for the LSWR London suburban traffic between 1863 and 1875 by Beyer Peacock of Manchester. Most of the class were withdrawn between 1886 and 1899 except three retained and based at Wadebridge for use on the tightly curved Wenford line. These engines were Nos. 298, 314 and 329, which later became BR Nos. 30587, 30585 and 30586 in that order after nationalisation in 1948. They lasted in traffic until 1962 after 88 years service. Two, numbers 30585 and 30587 survived into preservation and both are seen here together passing Charlies Gate on 27 December 2008 with a winter gala train to Bodmin General.

The Bodmin line's home based Beattie tank is No. 30587 which is owned by the National Railway Museum and which had spent many years on static display in the small railway museum at Buckfastleigh on South Devon Railway in Southern Green livery. I often looked at the engine in that museum and never thought I would see it restored and working again in Cornwall! It arrived at Buckfastleigh from store in 1978 and remained there until December 2001 when it was removed and sent to the Flour Mill workshops in the Forest of Dean for restoration to working order. This overhaul was largely funded by Bodmin and Wenford supporter Mr Alan Moore. The engine returned "home" to Cornwall at Bodmin in November 2002 as BR No. 30587 and has proved very popular on photographic charters and as a guest loco at various heritage lines around the country since. Here it is seen coming through the trees at Charlies Gate on 10 April 2005 with a mixed goods, a real recreation of the Wenford branch some 50 years earlier.

Opposite: Another view of No. 30587 on photo charter duty, this time on 20 October 2009 passing Westheath Road in glorious light with a mixed goods. It is truly remarkable that in the early years of the twenty-first century we are still able to witness such scenes.

Right: The two Beattie's are seen together again on 27 December 2008 passing St Lawrence on the climb from Boscarne Junction. No. 30585 is preserved at the Buckinghamshire Railway Museum, Quainton Road, Bucks and pays fairly frequent visits "home" to Cornwall. It too was restored to working order in the early years of the twenty-first century and the work also received kind financial support from Mr Alan Moore.

Only occasionally at special events does a single Beattie haul a passenger service due to the steep gradients and small size of the locomotives. However on 1 September 2006 No. 30587 rounds the sharp "Check Rail curve" on the approach to Bodmin General from Boscarne with a two coach passenger service.

A rear three quarters view of No. 30587 as it hauls a china clay train away from Bodmin Road and onto the branch on 24 March 2003.

Finally in this section we see No. 30587 departing Bodmin Road with a goods working on 16 October 2009 as former Wadebridge engineman Tony Hallworth looks out, probably still not believing he's doing just what he did for a job almost 50 years ago!

17. DREASON CURVE

By far the biggest engine in regular use on the line is big GWR 2-8-0T No. 4247. This engine was built in March 1916 as one of 165 members of its class which was principally designed for hauling heavy coal trains in the Welsh valleys. No. 4247 spent a period in "the valleys" but also worked in Cornwall on china clay trains including working over the gradient through Pinnock Tunnel (now a private road). The engine was withdrawn in April 1964 aged 48 years and was sent to Barry scrapyard. In April 1985 she left the scrapyard in the ownership of the 4247 Preservation Society and restoration was carried out at various sites around the country and re-entry to traffic came in September 2001 at the West Somerset Railway. The engine moved to Bodmin in September 2004 and had extensive work carried out early in 2005. The engine is now staying at the Bodmin line until at least 2022. Here the engine works hard up the steep gradient at Dreason on 3 May 2009. *Bernard Mills*

A trackside view of the T9
No. 30120 showing her
hauling a photo charter
recreation of a North
Cornwall line train around
the curve at Dreason on
8 October 2010.

A scene which just oozes
Wenford line atmosphere as
Beattie tank No. 30587
hauls a mixed goods
through Dreason Woods on
16 October 2009.

18. **DIESELS**

The Bodmin line also has a small fleet of diesels which are used for special enthusiasts days, engineering and works trains. The majority of classes represented are examples of types that worked in Cornwall in the past, so continuing the strong Cornish railway museum theme. The fleet includes locos from classes 33, 37 and 50 but does not include any of the much missed diesel hydraulics. To fill this gap the railway has on occasions had visiting diesel locos of these types. In June 1991 the railway hired in Hymek and Western locos from the Diesel and Electric Preservation Group at the West Somerset Railway. Here Hymek Type 3 No. D7017, in the attractive two tone green livery but with full yellow ends that the members of the class carried in BR service, drops downhill at Charlies Gate with a service for Bodmin Road. These locos were introduced in 1962 and due to BR standardisation policies all were withdrawn and scrapped by 1974 with the exception of four examples that have survived into preservation.

The first privately preserved mainline diesel in the UK was Warship diesel hydraulic No. D821 Greyhound, purchased from BR service in 1972 by a group of enthusiasts now known as the Diesel Traction Group. The Warships were another type of diesel hydraulic, that transmission system being preferred by the Western Region over diesel electric, that was introduced in 1958 as one of the first "pilot scheme" locomotives ordered for the modernisation of British Railways. The design was based on that of the German V200 type but built to the smaller British loading gauge. The class had all gone from mainline service by 1972, also as a result of BR standardisation and the decision to eliminate diesel hydraulics – which to many people was the final act of the old Great Western Railway. On 31 March 2001 D821 is seen leaving Bodmin General with a service to Boscarne whilst on a visit to the line, at the time the loco was carrying temporary nameplates "Cornwall". Also in this picture are the line's resident Class 20 in the foreground and in the background Class 50 No. 50042. *Classic Traction.*

The third type of mainline diesel hydraulic to survive into preservation is undoubtedly the most popular, following the huge enthusiast interest in their final workings in the mid 1970s. The Westerns, of which 74 were built between 1961 and 1963, are of a very attractive design – shame more modern loco designs don't come anywhere near this for aesthetics! The class achieved probably the largest following of any single class of loco, steam included, between 1974 and 1977 prior to the final end of the hydraulic era in mainline service. Happily one member of the class D1015 Western Champion has returned to the mainline for railtour use. There are seven examples in preservation and here we see Diesel and Electric Preservation Group/West Somerset Railway based D1010 Western Campaigner, then running as D1035 Western Yeoman in recognition of the contribution to its survival by Foster Yeoman Quarries, climbing past Charlies Gate in June 1991 in BR Green livery.

The class 50 diesel electrics were transferred to the Western Region from the West Coast mainline following electrification of that route in the mid 1970s to replace the Westerns. These powerful 2700 hp locos were the last 100mph design built for British Rail and were introduced in 1967. They have in turn been replaced by the HSTs on the mainline network and the class finally bowed out of mainline service in 1997 although no fewer than 19 of the original 50 have survived into preservation. The Bodmin Railway-based example is No. 50042 Triumph and it is seen here passing Cutmadoc on 5 April 2008. *Classic Traction*

During the 1950s and '60s BR introduced numerous Diesel Multiple Unit types to service on branch and mainline service. There was a variety of types including suburban and cross country configurations for service in different areas of the country. One of the last types of "First Generation" DMUs to remain in BR service, prior to replacement by modern Sprinter units, were the Class 108 two car sets and the Bodmin Railway has one unit in its care for use on off peak and land-cruise services. They are popular for these due to the good forward view for passengers sitting behind the driver. The unit is seen at Bodmin General. *Classic Traction*

19. CHARLIES GATE

Without doubt the most popular and well-known photographic location on the Bodmin line is Charlies Gate which lies just off the A38 road about ¾ mile from Bodmin Road. The location is so named, it is said, as the Royal Train has often been stabled there overnight in the past, and the access gate alongside the track, out into the small adjacent lane, has been used for "Royal guests" to exit the lineside. With the kind permission of the landowner many a good photograph of the railway has been taken from this section of the inside of the curve which is largely clear of vegetation etc. In this view we see 14xx class 0-4-2T No. 1450 on a short goods working amid the fresh colours of spring on 13 May 1997.

Opposite: Another, slightly longer, goods working with the South Devon Railway-based Prairie tank No. 5526 passing by on the fine spring afternoon of 19 April 2010. The contrast of how spring develops through just a few weeks is clear to see in these two images.

Opposite: If you venture up the hill from the lineside at Charlies Gate you are offered far reaching views along the Glynn Valley towards Liskeard, which is followed by the mainline, with the Bodmin branch passing by in the lower foreground. Here an almost timeless scene is created as Prairie No. 5552 hauls a short clay train up the grade towards Bodmin General on 18 October 2003.

Recent cutting back of lineside vegetation has now opened up views of trains on the east side of the line for early morning shots at this location when the sun is still on that side of the line. Just before 9.00 am on 8 October 2010 the T9 No. 30120 climbs past with an appropriately short passenger train in BR 1950s' Red/Cream livery now the standard colours of Bodmin Railway stock.

During the period of transition from Maroon to Red/Cream livery for Bodmin line stock, 2-8-0T No. 4247 takes a four-coach train up the grade past Charlies Gate on 8 April 2007. Such a short train is a very easy task for this powerful heavy goods locomotive. *Classic Traction*

Opposite: Another view of No. 5526 passing by with a goods working on 10 April 2010 taken from the east side of the line and which shows the lane running alongside the line in the background. Lineside vegetation clearance always allows more primroses to grow on the lineside in place of the brambles and other scrub, so a real environmental benefit is achieved from this work as well as to the railway itself.

A recreation of a North Cornwall line local service of the 1950s is seen passing Charlies Gate behind the T9 4-4-0 on 21 October 2010. Note the green-liveried PMV parcels van at the head of the train, so typical of such trains on the Southern Region's Devon and Cornwall lines (known as the Withered Arm) in that period.

20. THE T9

The elegant and graceful lines of the Drummond T9 design are seen to great effect here as No. 30120 runs round its train at Bodmin Parkway on 7 October 2010. The T9 class totalled 66 engines designed for the LSWR by Dugald Drummond and introduced in 1899. They were built at two works – the LSWR's own Nine Elms, London works and Dubbs & Co. works in Glasgow. The class became known as "Greyhounds" due to their good turn of speed on expresses. All survived through Southern Railway days but withdrawals commenced soon after nationalisation and 20 remained in service at the end of 1959 being used on lighter duties in the West Country. The last to be withdrawn was No. 30120 in 1963 and it was preserved for the national collection.

Below: No. 30120 was withdrawn from Exmouth Junction shed in 1961 but remained in stock and was given a heavy repair and returned to service in LSWR Green livery working service trains and specials. It was finally withdrawn in July 1963 but continued to work specials until October that year. Following periods in store around the country it was overhauled in the early 1980s and returned to steam in 1983 at the Mid Hants Railway. It moved to the Swanage Railway in 1991 until its boiler ticket expired in 1993 when it was moved to the Bluebell Railway where it remained as a static exhibit until 2009 when it moved to the Bodmin Railway and was given a full overhaul at the Flour Mill works in the Forest of Dean, largely funded by Mr Alan Moore. It was officially launched into traffic on 2 September 2010 and is seen here passing Charlies Gate with a launch day special working.

The class was equipped with an eight-wheel tender, which can be seen here and these became known as "Watercarts". Also note the shape of the waterspace is revealed, being shown by the cold water inside causing condensation on the tender sides. On 8 October 2010 the loco strides away from Bodmin Parkway with a photo charter.

With the driver working hard to keep the loco's large 6ft 7" driving wheels from slipping the T9 is worked through the trees and around Dreason curve shortly after departure from Bodmin Parkway on 8 October 2010.

A cold and frosty autumn morning allows the steam leaking from the engine's glands to envelop the engine as it hauls a charter train past Charlies Gate early on 21 October 2010.

Opposite: For me the winter period is by far the best for steam photography, with the crisp clear light and low sun angle combined with cool temperatures to enable the steam effects from the exhaust to be clearly visible. I'd headed down to Cornwall for a day's steam photography at the line's winter gala on 2 January 2010 and was pleasantly surprised to find a light dusting of snow in the Bodmin area on my arrival. A morning train from Bodmin Parkway makes a spectacular sight behind Prairie No. 5552.

Later that same day we see Beattie Well tank No. 30587 piloting Pannier No. 6435 round the check rail curve into Bodmin General with a train from Boscarne. The home signal sitting a danger alongside the train was not yet in service at the time of photograph!

The same combination of Nos. 30587 and 6435 is seen again, this time climbing round Quarry curve near the Walker Lines industrial estate with a train from Bodmin Parkway also on 2 January 2010. Note the snow still lying in the shadows in the foreground.

Still on that superb winter's day of 2 January 2010 we see an afternoon train from Bodmin Parkway working hard past Charlies Gate behind 64xx Pannier No. 6435. This engine had recently been purchased by the line from the Torbay and Dartmouth Railway.

During the period of transition from Maroon to Red/Cream liveried stock, Prairie No. 5552 heads a three-coach train from Bodmin Parkway past Charlies Gate on 27 December 2008.

22. COLESLOGGETT

The line's home based Pannier No. 4612 was out shopped in BR Black livery for the final six months of its ten year boiler ticket and for the autumn 2010 gala its identity was temporarily changed to former locally-based engine No. 4666. It is seen here passing Colesloggett Halt with a train for Bodmin General on 12 October 2010. *Classic Traction*

Recent tree clearance work in the Colesloggett area opened up several new vantage points for photographers (although this work is not done solely for this purpose!). The railway built the small halt here in preservation days and no station existed here in GWR/BR times. On 17 April 2010 GWR 2-8-0T No. 4247 is seen working up the grade with a Bodmin General-bound train.

A classic short pick up goods is seen heading past Colesloggett on 13 May 1997 behind 14xx tank No. 1450. Sadly this location is no longer possible for photographs due to re-growth of the lineside vegetation.

23. HAULING THE GOODS

The recreation of goods trains on country branch lines has to be one of the greatest sights on our heritage lines today and one which can perhaps more accurately than any other recreate a timeless scene. No. 5552 is seen heading a china clay train recreation up from Boscarne Junction near Pendewey on 18 October 2003.

A sight I cannot tire of is that of a little Beattie tank with a short goods train on the Bodmin line. Here No. 30587 runs round Quarry curve almost at the top of the climb from Bodmin Parkway with a goods …

... as the train passes we turn around and see the engine pick up a glint of the light as the train heads away towards Bodmin General. 10 April 2005.

Opposite: A shunting scene at a country branch line station is another sight that many thought had gone forever with the end of steam in the 1960s. However our heritage lines have restored many wagons as well as passenger coaches to recreate such scenes and here we watch No. 5552 shunting at Bodmin General on 1 September 2006.

A short train of open wagons is seen heading away from Boscarne Junction behind dock Pannier No. 1369 on 6 September 1996.

Also leaving Boscarne Junction and crossing the River Camel bridge is South Devon Railway-based Prairie No. 5526 with a mixed goods on 19 April 2010.

On the same day No. 5526 is seen further up the climb from Boscarne at Pendewey heading along some weed-strewn track typical of many branch lines in the later years of steam.

The Bodmin line is one of very few heritage lines to have experienced real rail freight work in the preservation era. The customer was long term supporter of the Bodmin line, Fitzgerald Lighting on the Walker Lines industrial estate in Bodmin who dispatched products regularly by rail. Wagons were tripped down from the factory along the heritage line to Bodmin Parkway and then shunted into an exchange siding for a BR diesel to collect later as part of the then Railfreight Distribution network. The traffic was lost to rail when the mainline operators decided the services did not pay and they were discontinued. The services were reintroduced with rail privatisation but this too ended after only a short period. Here the railway's class 10 diesel shunter D3452 in BR Black livery heads the three loaded wagons down to Bodmin Parkway on 4 June 1992. *Bernard Mills*

Opposite: Approximately half way up the climb from Boscarne Junction to Bodmin General is a popular lineside photographic location where access to the line (for those with lineside permits only) is fairly easy, adjacent to Westheath Road. Several different shots can be obtained here with the use of different lenses etc. Another unusual feature in recent years has been a colourful display of blue forget-me-nots covering the track in mid April. The blue carpet of flowers is clearly visible here as Prairies Nos. 5552 and 5526 doublehead a train up the grade on 18 April 2010.

With my lens set at 84mm I have been able to more tightly crop this shot of T9 No. 30120 working a photo charter formed of two coaches and two vans on 8 October 2010. The warm air of the day is making visible exhaust difficult, but the crew have managed to produce some grey coal smoke at just the right moment as another shovel full of coal is placed onto the fire.

A different longer distance view of the Westheath Road location obtained from a nearby hill and the use of a 300mm lens as No. 5552 heads a three coach train up the gradient on 2 January 2010.

25. SPECIAL EVENTS

The Bodmin and Wenford Railway, like most heritage lines, stages special events on a regular basis. These range from enthusiasts' galas to wartime weekends and Thomas the Tank/children's events. Concentrating here on enthusiasts' galas we first see a most unusual combination of the railway's two Port of Par shunters, Alfred and Judy, hauling two brake vans up the steep grade past Charlies Gate on 3 April 2009. These two very low locomotives were specially built for use in Par Docks and to be able to work clay wagons under the Great Western mainline which passes over the line linking the docks to St Blazey yard. They are often referred to as "The Flying Bufferbeams". *Bernard Mills*

Visiting engines are often a part of gala events and on 22 March 2008 Terrier 0-6-0T No. 3 "Bodiam" from the Kent and East Sussex Railway pilots home-based Pannier No. 4612 on a train from Bodmin Parkway a little way past Charlies Gate where the line is right beside the A38 trunk road. Evidence of recent cutting back had opened up this shot at the time. *Classic Traction*

Bluebells are in evidence as GWR 2-8-0T No. 4247 heads a gala service past Charlies Gate on 3 May 2009.

Opposite: On 18 April 2010 Prairies Nos. 5526 and 5552 head upgrade past Quarry curve with a train for Bodmin General formed of appropriate Red/Cream Mk.1 stock.

Continuing the theme of enthusiast galas we now look at a number of visiting engines that have graced the Bodmin line in recent years, many of which would most certainly not have ventured onto a Great Western branch line in GWR or BR days. First we see a very unusual visitor in the form of LNER V2 2-6-2 No. 60800 Green Arrow from the National Railway Museum, York, then in the very smart BR Lined Green livery, leaving Bodmin Parkway on 2 May 1999. The engine was visiting Cornwall on railtour duty and spent the weekend between railtours stabled on the line and in use for a special weekend. *Bernard Mills*

Opposite: A further view of the V2 on 2 May 1999, this time passing Charlies Gate with a five-coach train of matching Maroon coaches. *Bernard Mills*

For many years Bulleid West Country Pacific No. 34007 Wadebridge was appropriately based on the line for its long restoration from scrapyard condition by its owning group with some work carried out by the workshop staff at Bodmin. It was always clear that the engine was really too big for regular use on the line and so despite its local name and historic connections with the railways of North Cornwall, it was moved to the Mid Hants Railway where it is based to this day. However on its initial return to steam the engine did work trains on the branch for a limited time and on 29 October 2006 No. 34007 passes Charlies Gate with a return to steam special. *Classic Traction*

A former Southern Region visitor perhaps more in keeping with a branch line, was Ivatt class 2 tank No. 41312 (here numbered as former local engine 41316 for a photo charter) seen passing Charlies Gate with a single coach and van, so typical of trains on the old line from Halwill Junction to Torrington. *Bernard Mills*

Following its recent return to traffic following overhaul, and before heading home to the West Somerset Railway, large Prairie No. 4160 visited several heritage lines including Bodmin. On 1 September 2006 the engine passes Charlies Gate with a two coach local train working.

Our parade of visiting engines passing Charlies Gate continues with Collett 0-6-0 No. 3205 heading past with a short goods train. This engine is based at the South Devon Railway. *Bernard Mills*

The final visitor we see at Charlies Gate is another former GWR engine in the form of 0-6-2T No. 5619 from the Telford Steam Railway, heading the 17.15 train from Bodmin Parkway to Bodmin General on 4 September 2009. *Classic Traction*

27. THROUGH THE COUNTRYSIDE

Lineside bluebells make a colorful foreground to this shot of No. 6435 and its autocoach at Westheath on 10 May 2011.

Very much a "train in the landscape" shot as No. 5552 climbs up from Boscarne at Lavendon on 2 January 2010.

The wooded Glynn Valley in late summer forms the backdrop to this shot of No. 4160 heading two coaches and a goods van towards Bodmin General near Charlies Gate on 1 September 2006.

This shot perhaps shows how a familiar location can look quite different by varying your view point: we are back at Charlies Gate on 21 October 2010 for the T9 heading a North Cornwall line local train recreation.

A nice BR combination of Prairie No. 5526 and Pannier No. 6435 doubleheading a train from Bodmin Parkway past Charlies Gate on 18 April 2010.

Opposite: The almost unbelievable sight of the two Beattie Well tanks, Nos. 30585 & 30587, working together in preservation in matching BR Black livery. The two engines have a combined age of 275 years! Here they are passing Westheath on 27 December 2008 with a train from Boscarne.

Another classic country branchline scene is created in deepest Cornwall as we close with this image of Pannier No.4666 hauling a goods away from Boscarne Junction on 9 May 2011.